GLADIATORS

GLADIATORS

ODYSSEYS

RACHAEL HANEL

CREATIVE EDUCATION · CREATIVE PAPERBACKS

Published by Creative Education and Creative Paperbacks
P.O. Box 227, Mankato, Minnesota 56002
Creative Education and Creative Paperbacks
are imprints of The Creative Company
www.thecreativecompany.us

Design by Graham Morgan
Art direction by Tom Morgan

Images by Alamy Stock Photo/Album, 50; Getty Images/Alexander Sorokopud, 17, Archive Photos, 67, Arctic-Images, 73, duncan1890, 37, Halfdark, 24, mikroman6, 8, 22, 46, Stefano Bianchetti, 28, ZU_09, 60; Pexels/Luiz Valerio Trindade, 54; Unsplash/Hasmik Ghazaryan Olson, 12; Wikimedia Commons/F. Mattej artist, Fausto and Felix Niccolini editors, 32, Francesco Netti, 4–5, Howard Pyle, 2, Jean-Léon Gérôme, 38, 62, José Moreno Carbonero, 42, Klaus D. Peter, Wiehl, Germany, 6, Nicolao Landucci, 10, Poniol60, 68–69, public domain, cover, 26, Richard Croft, 49, TimeTravelRome, 18

Library of Congress Cataloging-in-Publication Data
Names: Hanel, Rachael, author.
Title: Gladiators / Rachael Hanel.
Description: Mankato, Minnesota : Creative Education and Creative Paperbacks, [2026] | Series: Odysseys in combat | Includes bibliographical references and index. | Audience: Ages 12–15 years | Audience: Grades 7–9 | Summary: "Prepare for battle alongside the warriors of Ancient Rome called gladiators by learning about their weapons, combat skills, and reasons for fighting. Includes a glossary, sidebars, index, and further resources"—Provided by publisher.
Identifiers: LCCN 2024049691 (print) | LCCN 2024049692 (ebook) | ISBN 9798889896463 (lib. bdg.) | ISBN 9781682778128 (paperback) | ISBN 9798889897262 (ebook)
Subjects: LCSH: Gladiators—Rome—History—Juvenile literature. | Rome—Social life and customs—Juvenile literature. | Rome—History—Juvenile literature.
Classification: LCC GV35 .H36 2026 (print) | LCC GV35 (ebook) | DDC 796.850937—dc23/eng/20241211 7
LC record available at https://lccn.loc.gov/2024049691
LC ebook record available at https://lccn.loc.gov/2024049692

Printed in India

Ancient artwork depicting a gladiator fight

CONTENTS

Introduction

From the beginning of time, wherever groups of people have lived together, they have also fought among themselves. Some have fought for control of basic necessities—food, water, and shelter—or territory. Others have been spurred to fight by religious differences. Still others have fought solely for sport. Throughout the ages, some fighters have taken up arms willingly. Others have been forced into battle. For all, however, the ultimate goal has always been victory.

OPPOSITE: At its height, the Roman Empire commanded nearly half a million fighting soldiers.

OPPOSITE Many gladiators who entered an arena to fight never came out alive.

Gladiators—big men armed with glinting swords and strong shields—fought not for land, wealth, or treasure, but to entertain the masses. The slaves, criminals, hostages, and occasional volunteers who made up gladiator ranks served one purpose only: to perform for the Roman emperor and the public. These warriors, who lived 2,000 years ago, were the ancient equivalent of modern-day sports heroes, their mere appearance in large theaters eliciting frenzied screams of anticipation from massive crowds. Although little is known about specific Roman gladiators, what is known is that each faced one of two fates: kill or be killed. Even if a gladiator was skilled enough to slay an opponent in battle, he might not be so lucky the next time.

The Rise of a Fighter

Gladiators emerged at a time when one of the greatest empires in history—the Roman Empire—ruled much of the world. At the height of its power, the Roman Empire encompassed most of Europe, Britain, northern Africa, and Asia Minor (present-day Turkey). The empire dates back to 753 BCE and finally collapsed some 1,000 years later, in 476 CE. At the same time, civilized societies flourished in Africa, India, and Asia. But none rivaled the Roman Empire's sheer size and power.

OPPOSITE: Ruins of the largest amphitheater in the world still stand in Rome, Italy. The Colosseum opened in 80 CE and was used for spectator events such as gladiator battles.

Romans influenced everything from architecture, art, and theater to politics and philosophy. The city of Rome served as the empire's crown jewel.

Kings dominated Rome's early years, until the last king was removed from the throne in 509 BCE. For the next several centuries, the Roman **senate** elected rulers in one of the first-ever **democratic** systems. Rome grew through a series of military conquests—first in Italy, then south to Greece. Through the centuries, Rome's leaders ordered bloody attacks and marched over France, Britain, and Persia. Soldiers fought sea battles and conquered Egypt and Carthage in northern Africa.

Eventually, Rome's democratic system of government disappeared under willful **dictators**, such as Julius Caesar (100–44 BCE), who claimed absolute power. Augustus Caesar (63 BCE–14 CE), Julius Caesar's son, became the first Roman emperor in 27 BCE. From that point until the empire ended roughly 500 years later, 86 emperors ruled the territory. Some acted justly and fairly, while others thrived on cruelty and violence.

Gladiators first appeared around the year 264 BCE. The first gladiatorial fight occurred at the funeral of a **nobleman**. It was the revitalization of a custom practiced among the Etruscan people, a pre-Roman society that lived in Italy. The Etruscans believed that the sacrifice of a human life at a funeral would please the gods. The Roman public enjoyed watching the fight, and soon powerful citizens seeking public favor staged even more funeral fights. High-ranking Romans created more elaborate shows to compete with one another, and men called *lanistae* organized fights for a fee. They traveled around the empire to show off their skilled fighters. It soon became a thriving business to train gladiators and put on fighting shows.

Before long, the emperor himself realized that he could increase his standing among the public if he sponsored grand spectacles featuring gladiator competitions. Julius Caesar was the first leader to organize these shows himself rather than having the *lanistae* do so. He also offered bountiful feasts as part of the celebration. Augustus Caesar then brought all gladiator fights under his direct control. For the next couple of centuries, the

Statue of a Roman emperor

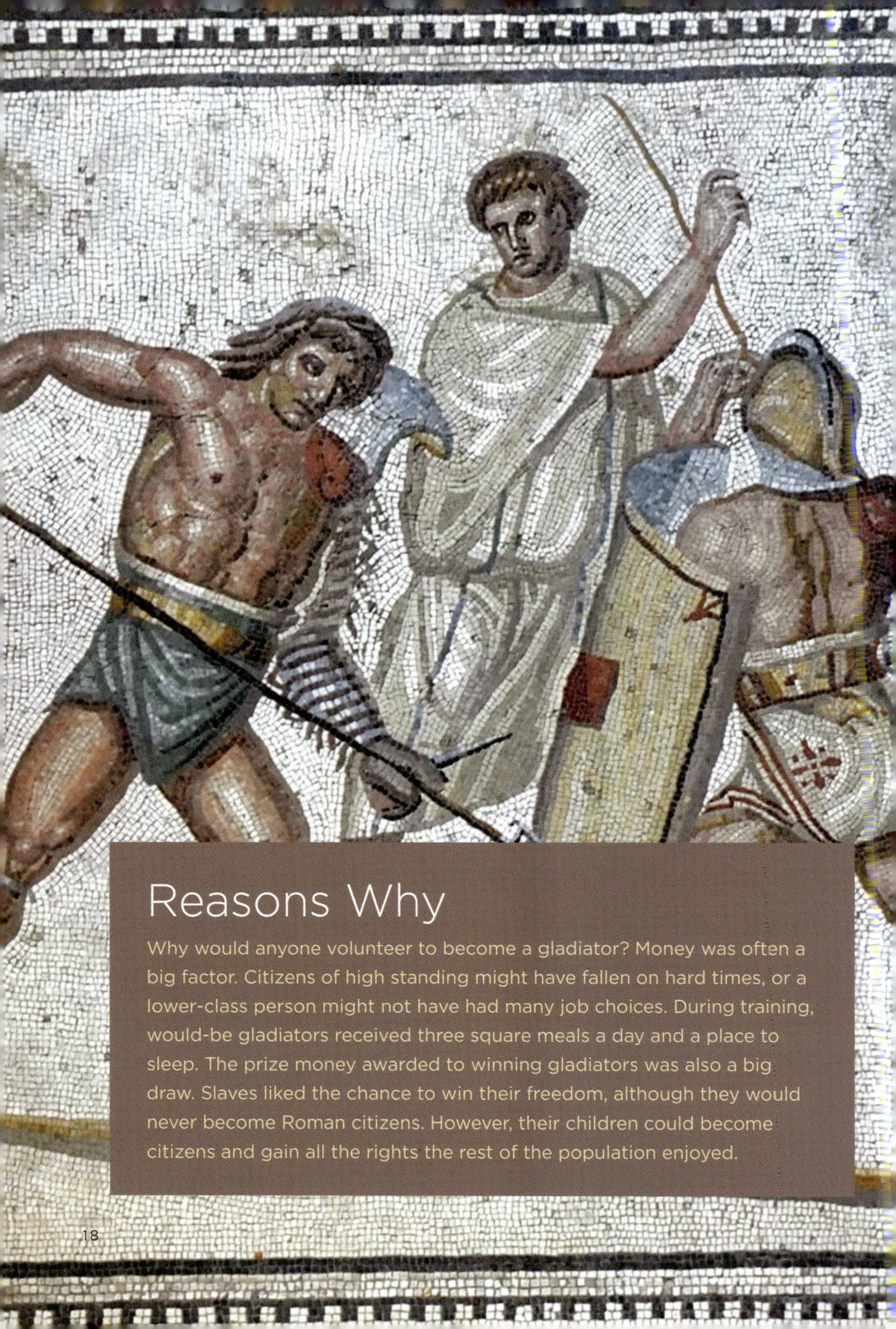

Reasons Why

Why would anyone volunteer to become a gladiator? Money was often a big factor. Citizens of high standing might have fallen on hard times, or a lower-class person might not have had many job choices. During training, would-be gladiators received three square meals a day and a place to sleep. The prize money awarded to winning gladiators was also a big draw. Slaves liked the chance to win their freedom, although they would never become Roman citizens. However, their children could become citizens and gain all the rights the rest of the population enjoyed.

fights remained a central theme in Roman life and grew more violent, elaborate, and deadly.

Gladiators were pulled from the lowest rungs of society. Enslaved people, hostages, and criminals served unwillingly as gladiators. Occasionally, a daring (some might say crazy) man volunteered. Sometimes noblemen even offered themselves as gladiators to gain favor with the public. But for most gladiators, cruel fate landed them in this position. Many would-be gladiators came from the Roman Empire's conquered lands. When the military secured victory in places such as Germany, Britain, Egypt, and northern Africa, the native people became prisoners of war. They either marched, chained together, back to Rome, or boarded cramped ships to sail across the Mediterranean Sea to the city. In Rome, the hostages were auctioned off as slaves for Roman citizens.

The biggest and strongest males were tagged to become gladiators.

Sometimes enslaved people who had been sold to Roman citizens eventually became gladiators as well. Romans who tired of their slaves could get rid of them by forcing them into gladiator training. Slaves who tried to run away or rebel also were sent away to training.

Criminals often were forced to fight, too. Even before the rise of gladiators, the Romans had a long history of sentencing criminals to cruel deaths. In the early days of the Roman Empire, soldiers forced criminals into public arenas, where they were either killed by an executioner or fed to a wild beast. As gladiator fights became more popular, criminals did not receive swift and certain deaths but instead were sentenced to train and fight as gladiators.

No one envied a gladiator's life. Training was intense, and every time gladiators marched into an arena, they knew it could be the last time. A gladiator with many wins under his belt had just as much of a chance of losing as a novice fighter. The losers didn't simply go home to sulk; a loss almost always meant death.

When they weren't fighting one another, gladiators tried to live normal lives. A gladiator might marry and have

children. Enslaved people, who (along with criminal fighters) were confined to their training schools, might try to earn enough prize money to buy their freedom and the freedom of their families. But this goal always carried a huge risk: The gladiator might not live long enough to earn the needed money.

Few gladiators lived to old age. But those who did were the most successful in the fighting circuit. They were strong and powerful and garnered wins every time they stepped into the arena. The public loved these men. Each time successful

Modern Gladiators

In 1997, it was discovered that prison guards at Corcoran State Prison in California were staging "gladiator fights" among prisoners in outside exercise yards. These fights became regular entertainment at the prison, and guards pitted men from rival gangs against each other. One guard reportedly acted as an announcer, while other guards bet on the events. The fights turned deadly—a total of seven inmates died in prison-yard fights between 1989 and 1994. Two guards finally reported their colleagues' actions, but a jury **acquitted** eight guards of federal charges, citing a lack of evidence of wrongdoing.

gladiators marched in front of Roman crowds, they were greeted with deafening roars of approval, and the men soaked it up. When a successful gladiator retired, gladiator schools often competed for his teaching skills. At training schools, he taught younger men how to fight, earning a respected place not only in the gladiator community but in society.

Although winning gladiators might draw fans, most gladiators were detested by the public. Ordinary Romans viewed themselves as superior to gladiators and welcomed the chance to watch the fighters' bloody and violent deaths. Occasionally, an especially colorful gladiator might gain favor with the public even if he hadn't been successful in battle. Romans might compete for pieces of his clothing or other objects he owned, and wealthy people might have artists create vases or mosaics decorated with his image. But this type of gladiator was rare.

8
9
10
11
13
15
16
17
18
19
21
22
23
26
27
28
ROMA
30
33

Blades and Armor at the Ready

The Romans divided their gladiators into many different categories; each fighter wore a different uniform and wielded a different weapon. The groups sometimes represented various enemies of Rome. That way, when these gladiators entered the arena, they played the role of the "enemy," much to the crowd's delight.

OPPOSITE: Uniforms and weapons of Roman soldiers and gladiators were as varied as the men's duties and responsibilities.

Despite the differences among groups, most gladiators used some type of shield and sword (the Latin word *gladius* means "sword"). Their short swords featured sharp sides all around and were most effective in hand-to-hand combat. A strong gladiator throwing all of his weight behind a quick thrust of the sword could deliver sudden death.

Few gladiators wore much armor—usually simply leg guards and helmets. Often, their chests and upper arms stayed bare. The reason for this was practical: the less armor a gladiator wore, the easier he was to kill. What little armor a gladiator did wear, along with his weapons and equipment, was supplied for free by gladiator training schools—just one small perk to help atone for the grave dangers gladiators faced.

For the Samnites, the first gladiators to emerge in the Roman Empire, equipment included a short sword and a large shield that protected them from head to knee. Samnites, who took their name from the Samnium people, early enemies of Rome, wore leather or metal bands around their arms and one leg. A large helmet covered their entire head, their eyes peering out through two eye holes, and a crest and feather adorned the helmet's top.

Another category of gladiator, the Hoplomachi, was styled after the Greeks, a frequent Roman opponent. Hoplomachi also wielded a small sword and large shield. They wrapped their shins and thighs in leather bands for protection from dagger slices. In their left hand, they grasped their shield, and their right arm was enveloped in armor. Like the Samnites, Hoplomachi wore helmets that covered their head and vulnerable neck area.

The Mirmillo gladiator went by the name of "fish man" because images of fish adorned the hat-like helmet that left his face exposed. He bore a short sword, and his shield was round, unlike the others. He kept his legs bare and depended on his shield for lower body protection. On the arm that didn't hold the shield, the Mirmillo wore leather or metal, much like the Gauls, a tribe from France.

In fights, the Mirmillo often found himself up against the Retiarius, who carried no sword or shield. Instead, the Retiarius relied upon a net for his weapon, using it to snare and entangle his opponents. Weights lined the net's outer edges, so when it was thrown, it descended quickly over the opponent. The Retiarius also carried a three-pointed spear called a trident. When his opponent became tangled in the net, the Retiarius stabbed him with the trident. The Retiarius went mostly unarmored, except for metal covering an arm. He wore no helmet,

Just Another Fighter

Besides protecting a gladiator's head, a helmet served another important purpose: It rendered the fighter unrecognizable. In gladiator training schools, students practiced for years alongside other students. Because they shared some common bonds, many became friends. If, in the ring, they saw that they were pitted against a good friend, they might have simply laid down their arms and refused to fight. Although they might have been killed as a result, in their minds, this would have been better than killing a friend. A helmet provided anonymity, which helped to **dehumanize** the fighters and meant that the fights would go on.

just a headband and could move more quickly than other gladiators because of his light weight. The Retiarius was similar to the Lacquerii fighter, who used a **noose** to capture opponents.

The Retiarius also often fought the Secutor, who carried a sword and a large shield that covered him nearly from head to toe. A metal plate protected his lower left leg, and the arm bearing the sword sported armor from fingertip to shoulder. Unlike some other fighters, Secutors wore a rounded helmet instead of one with a rectangular or pointed top—the curve allowed the net of the Retiarius to slide off. Secutors were also called "chasers" because they often ran after fleet-footed opponents in the arena.

The Thracian, named after fighters in northern Greece, held the smallest shield, a rounded one that didn't cover much. His sword was large and curved to inflict more bodily harm. His leg guards stretched from the ankle to the top of the thigh. Metal covered one arm, and the top of his helmet was often decorated with a **griffin**. Thracians usually battled another armored gladiator, usually either a Samnite or Mirmillo.

Although most gladiators fought in hand-to-hand combat, others specialized in more elaborate battles. Gladiators who raced around an arena in chariots were called Essedarii. Chariots were made small and lightweight in order to move quickly. The chariot driver cracked a whip at anything in sight, while his teammates used spears to attack opponents, also in chariots.

In the early days, gladiator fights took place wherever there was room to fight—usually an open square. When the fighting's popularity increased, gladiators moved to public **forums**. There, temporary stands were erected for the public and taken down as soon as the bout was over. When the emperor decreed that gladiator fights would be under his control, more permanent buildings were constructed. These buildings were called amphitheaters, and they featured a stage with seating on all sides. That way, everyone had a good view.

Gladiators fought on the floor of the amphitheater, and the seats rose high from that point. The emperor, royalty, famous politicians, and the wealthy claimed ringside seats. The middle class sat up from them, and the poorest people sat in the upper rows or stood on the very top walkways. Large canvas awnings shielded wealthier attendees from the blazing sun, and fountains sometimes sprayed a light mist over the crowd on hot days. Below the stands, the floor of the amphitheater was covered with sand, which quickly absorbed blood and could easily be replaced with fresh sand.

The largest and most famous amphitheater in Roman history was the Colosseum in Rome, which still stands today. The structure, which opened in 80 CE with 100 straight days of animal hunts and gladiator shows, could seat an estimated 50,000 spectators. Beneath the Colosseum, an enormous network of tunnels and rooms snaked through the two-level basement. This network allowed for a variety of special effects. For example, trap doors opened from the basement into the arena's floor; this way, wild animals seemed to pop up directly from the floor. Sections of the floor could be lowered, decorated with elaborate scenes like a play's stage, and then raised back up to provide colorful backdrops to the fights and animal hunts. The basement also held rooms dedicated to first aid, weapons storage, and a morgue.

Man's Best Friend

A runaway slave named Androcles (c. first century CE) is said to have been one of only a few men who left the arena alive after facing a lion. When the Emperor Caligula asked Androcles why the lion had acted warmly toward him, the answer was amazing: Androcles said that after running away from his would-be captors, he hid in a cave, where he encountered a lion with a thorn in its paw. Androcles removed the thorn, and the lion remained faithful to him. Later, both man and beast were captured in separate instances, and fate brought them together. The lion remembered Androcles and spared his life.

Fighting to the Death

Gladiators might spend years training for just one day in the arena. As gladiator fights became more common, emperors recognized that well-trained fighters put on better shows for the adoring public.

OPPOSITE: Wounded gladiators often gestured to the crowd for a show of mercy.

Soon, formal gladiator training schools opened. Strict teachers—men who had fought as gladiators and lived to tell about it—handed out tough punishments to trainees. They successfully transformed slaves and captives into brutal fighting machines who took pride in their societal roles. The teachers made gladiators-in-training believe they were part of an elite group. Only if a trainee studied hard and practiced long hours would he have any chance of survival in the arena, so it was to his benefit to become the best gladiator possible.

At first, new recruits learned to fight using wooden swords, striking straw bales or scarecrows. They learned fencing skills and underwent intense physical training. Later, recruits graduated to iron weapons that were heavy but kept blunt to prevent serious harm. Teachers also set aside time for lectures, recounting their exploits and describing their

Gladiator Art

Mosaics featuring gladiators in combat figured prominently in ancient homes of wealthy people. Archeologists discovered a large mosaic in Libya, a northern African country once part of the Roman Empire. The five large panels of the glass and stone mosaic spread more than 30 feet (9.1 meters), and its depictions are gory: A slain gladiator's head tilts backward in one panel, while in another a gladiator stands victorious over his dead opponent. Gladiator art has been found engraved on lamps and painted on large walls as murals as well.

techniques to the men sitting before them. A gladiator usually trained for three years before his first fight.

Some schools—a combination of prison camps and training centers—were run by private individuals, but emperors controlled other schools, where gladiators were hand-picked to fight for special occasions. Julius Caesar owned a school south of Rome, near the city of Capua, that had enough armor for 5,000 gladiators. Four schools were located within Rome itself, and the largest of these was connected to the Colosseum via an underground tunnel.

OPPOSITE Although they fought one another, many gladiators considered themselves part of a brotherhood.

Under the most ambitious emperors, gladiator fights were held dozens of times per year, often on holidays so that everyone could attend. Most fights followed the same general pattern. The public woke up early on the morning of a fight in anticipation of the big event. A gladiator fight was an all-day affair, with many different festivities, all leading up to the main attraction: the gladiators.

The day was a social occasion for the public. Early in the morning, as the crowd started to filter into the amphitheater, excited noise filled the streets. Merchants hawked their wares on tables outside, buyers sought bargains, and men and women gabbed among themselves. Before the fights started, spectators bought food from vendors and placed bets on which gladiators they thought would win.

An elaborate arena parade started the show. Musicians and dancers led the entertainment. They were followed by exotic animals—such as elephants, tigers, lions, and leopards—that the Romans had captured from faraway lands. The animals were dressed in fancy costumes and draped with flowers. After the parade, priests entered the arena and prayed to the many gods the Romans worshipped. Then the emperor and his court entered their private viewing area, stood up, and waved to the crowd. Only after the emperor and his family were seated did the games begin.

First, wild animals were released into the arena and hunted by skilled archers. Then it was time for the animal-versus-human fights, as men called Bestiarii battled lions, tigers, and bears. The Bestiarii were armed only with long spears. Some of the animals were killed by other animals, others were stabbed by Bestiarii, but a number of animals clawed and mauled Bestiarii to death. Only a few Bestiarii walked out of the arena alive.

Around midday, workers tossed numbered balls into the crowd to give away goods. Spectators might win meat, flour, animals, or even prizes as big as houses, slaves, or land. No doubt the scramble to grab a ball and win a prize became a violent struggle in itself. As the people in the stands were distracted by the prize giveaway, men worked on the floor of the arena below, clearing away dead bodies and spreading fresh sand.

In the afternoon, the first group of gladiators appeared. These were lower-ranking gladiators—common criminals or enslaved people forced to fight. This whetted the audience's appetite for the real performance to come. The real gladiators made a grand entrance later in the afternoon and evening. They marched into the arena to the sounds of trumpets, holding their heads high and relishing the praise coming from the thousands in

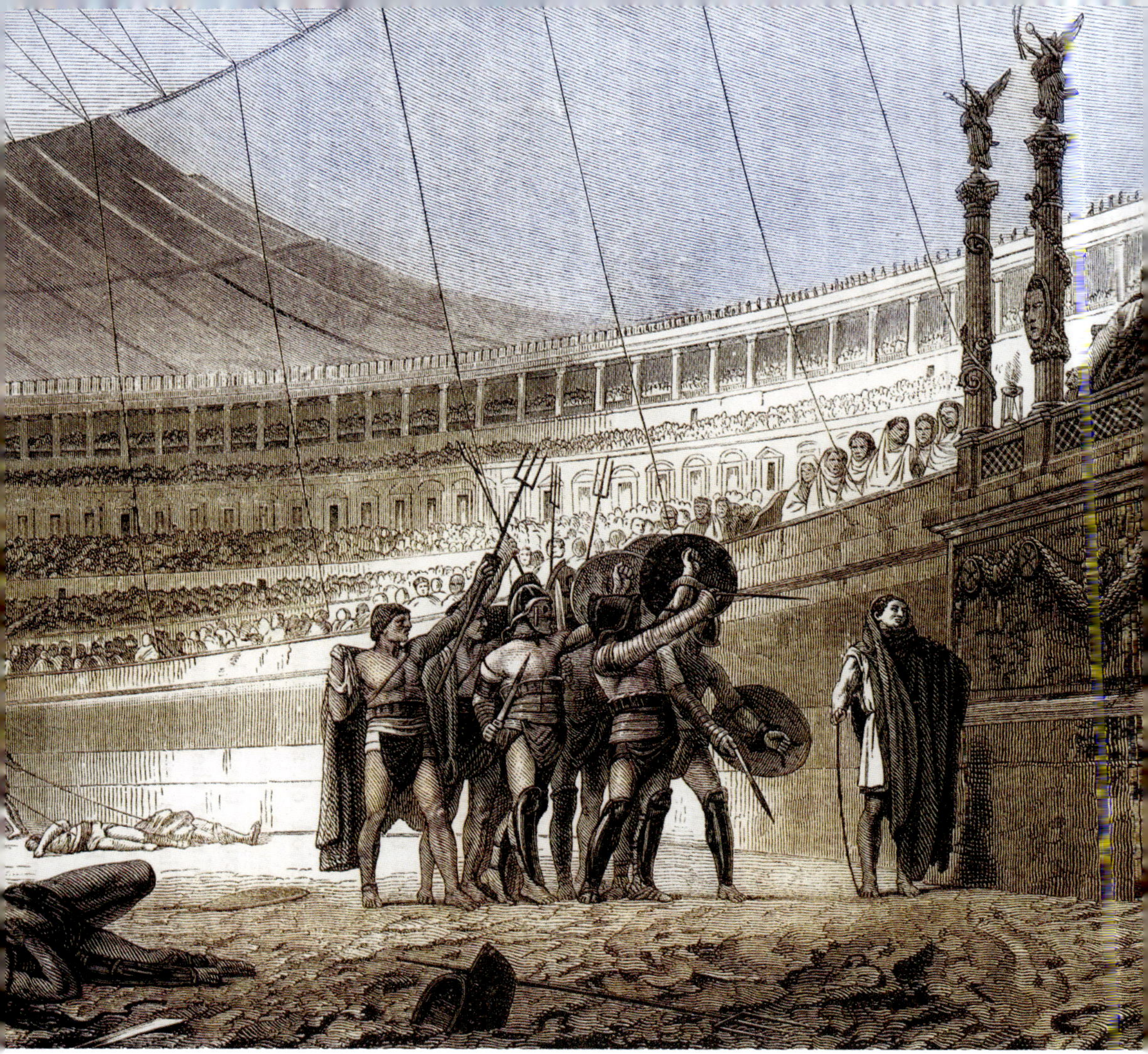

attendance. The warriors stopped before the emperor's throne and chanted, "We who are about to die salute you."

Then the fights began, with gladiators battling both one-on-one and as teams. Swords clashed against the metal of other swords and shields. Well-trained muscles rippled in the sun. The fighters' **agility** and skill awed the crowd. Gladiators spun around, trying to avoid the slice of a blade or the throw of a net. It didn't take long—usually only 10 to 15 minutes—before gladiators thudded to the ground, wounded in the stomach, head, or chest.

A fallen gladiator raised the first finger on his left hand, the traditional sign of mercy. The emperor usually decided the fighter's fate. More often than not, the emperor turned to the crowd for a decision. A popular gladiator might elicit sympathy from the audience if he gave a particularly brave fight. In that case, the crowd shouted "*Mitte*!" ("Let him go!") The emperor then turned down his thumb, which meant the gladiator would be allowed to leave the arena alive.

Most audiences didn't display such sympathy, though. Often they shouted "*Iugula*!" ("Kill him!") The emperor then gave a thumbs-up signal, and the gladiator accepted his fate. His victorious opponent delivered one fatal blow, usually to the neck. At the end of the day, the most popular gladiators fought each other; this was what the crowd had been waiting for. These fighters were the largest and strongest in all the empire. Each might have dozens of victories already. Those who lost their battles might be granted immunity by the emperor and decide to retire. For others, their previous victories didn't count for anything, and they lost their lives.

Ancient Doping

It seems that the use of performance-enhancing drugs by athletes is not a new phenomenon. Gladiators often ingested different types of herbs and drugs before competitions. Some used **stimulants**, such as caffeine, or other types of drugs, such as alcohol. Others turned to more lethal substances such as strychnine and nitroglycerine. Both are stimulants when taken in very small doses, but larger doses are poisonous and even deadly. The drug **opium** also was used. These supplements didn't ensure victory, but they probably helped gladiators combat fatigue and reduce injury.

F.186
F.185.

The Bravest and the Best

For six centuries, gladiator fights were an important part of Roman life, and during that time, hundreds of thousands of gladiators entered arenas. Most didn't leave alive. Because gladiator fights took place 2,000 years ago, almost all the fighters have been forgotten. However, information about a few gladiators survives thanks to archeological discoveries of artwork, bones, and gravestone inscriptions, along with rare historical written accounts.

OPPOSITE: The first gladiators fought with little and left little behind to remember them by when they died.

Perhaps most famous of all was a former slave and gladiator-in-training named Spartacus (c. 109–71 BCE). Spartacus is thought to have been born in Thrace, part of modern-day Greece. No one knows exactly how he became a slave. He may have originally been a Roman soldier who rebelled, ran away, and was later captured and enslaved. However it happened, Spartacus was forced to attend a gladiator training school in Capua. In 73 BCE, he escaped, along with 70 to 80 other gladiators-in-training. The runaways found an isolated spot on Mount Vesuvius, a volcano just south of Capua, and planned their escape from Italy, hoping to eventually gain their freedom.

The Roman army descended upon Spartacus and his followers on the mountain, but Spartacus was able to lead his army down the other side. He continued to stay one step ahead of the Romans and soon recruited 70,000 slaves, mostly from rural areas. His immense army crushed the Roman forces sent to stop the rebellion. As word of Spartacus's exploits grew, more and more enslaved people joined him. At the height of the rebellion, in 72 BCE, Spartacus was estimated to have had 120,000 followers. The slave army pushed the Roman army back across most of southern Italy and eventually threatened to descend upon Rome and assume power. Roman officials continued to try to thwart the revolt, and in 71 BCE, Spartacus and his followers were finally defeated in a major battle in southern Italy. The Roman army killed Spartacus and crucified an estimated 6,000 of his followers.

Spartacus never actually made it to the arena, where many gladiators died in their first fights. Gladiators were

Big Events

Archeological digs prove that gladiator fights were popular throughout the Roman Empire, extending from the capital into the empire's vast holdings. Ruins from a first-century amphitheater were recovered in the 1990s in a section of London, England. Evidence shows that the arena could seat 6,000 to 7,000 people—in a city that had a population of 20,000. That means one of every three people in the city could have attended the gladiator fights. To put that into perspective, a sporting event in New York City, with a population of roughly 8.2 million people, would attract 2.7 million!

happy to survive one fight and fought desperately to continue their winning ways. If they were lucky enough to win again and again, they could even possibly retire and live to old age. But some winning gladiators chose not to retire because their successes made them wildly popular, and they thrived on the attention. The gladiator Flamma ("The Flame") was one such case. Flamma originated from Syria, although it's not known when, and was perhaps forced into slavery and into a gladiator school. Flamma fought as a Secutor, so his common opponent was a Retiarius, and he successfully fought off the net time and time again. Fighters who exhibited great skill and bravery were presented with a wooden baton, called a *rudius*, which granted them early retirement. Flamma received the *rudius* not once, not twice, not three times, but an incredible four times. Each time

IF THEY WERE LUCKY ENOUGH TO WIN AGAIN AND AGAIN, THEY COULD EVEN POSSIBLY RETIRE AND LIVE TO OLD AGE.

he received it, he chose to return to the arena. He was killed in his 22nd fight at the age of 30.

Besides earning the opportunity to retire, famous and successful gladiators had the chance to receive riches from the emperor or be immortalized in artwork. The emperor Nero (37–68 CE) took a liking to the gladiator Spiculus (c. first century CE) and awarded him a palace and other property. When Nero was deposed by the Romans in 68 CE and faced certain death, he reportedly sought the hand of Spiculus, who could kill him quickly. Not finding Spiculus, Nero instead committed suicide. Spiculus must have been quite famous, for his likeness adorns Roman artwork. A glass gladiator cup found in France and dating from 50 to 80 CE features an image of Spiculus and seven other gladiators. The cup suggests that even when gladiator fights took place in Rome, word of their battles spread throughout the empire.

While most gladiators were unknown before they entered the arena, occasionally famous Romans—even an emperor—might step into the ring. The emperor Commodus (161–192 CE) was rumored to be the illegitimate son of a gladiator. Commodus claimed to be a great gladiator fighter, participating in anywhere from 300 to 1,000 fights, although he no doubt inflated the numbers to make himself appear tougher. Of course, Commodus won his fights—his opponents didn't want to injure or kill the emperor for fear of punishment or execution.

Commodus dressed like the god Hercules and took a particular liking to fighting wild animals. For every successful fight, he paid himself one million sesterces (gold coins). In comparison, an average Roman might earn just 1,000 sesterces in a year. Commodus was considered a ruthless emperor who spent time with his **harem** of women and neglected state duties. He was killed by a champion wrestler named Narcissus (c. 100s CE), a murder perhaps ordered by one of Commodus's mistresses.

Although gladiatorial games were the domain of men, women fought in the arena, too. Historians studying the Roman Empire have found vague references to women's fights in ancient writings. A female fighter, or gladiatrix, was known to fight not only other women but wild animals as well. One story surrounding a particular pair of women gladiators survives only through a piece of art.

A marble slab in the British Museum depicts the female fighters Amazon and Achillia (both c. first or second century CE). They are known to be women because they are pictured shirtless and one wears her hair in a long braid, a decidedly female fashion. Other than that, however, these fighters appear similar to their male counterparts. They wield shields and swords, appearing to fight with as much intensity as men. One wears what looks to be a wrapped-leather arm guard, and their helmets rest at their feet. The carving indicates that both women were given a **reprieve** by the crowd. They somehow gained enough favor while fighting to be allowed to live.

Decline of a Warrior

By the first century CE, gladiator fights were still bloody and violent but a little less spectacular. It became harder for emperors to put on the original, dazzling fights that had marked the early days of the contests. Overwhelmed by the vast size of the empire, emperors found it more difficult to collect the money needed to stage fantastic productions.

OPPOSITE: Those who practiced Christianity were persecuted in ancient Rome and often thrown to wild animals in arenas for entertainment.

Watching Violence

A closer look at the Roman Empire can offer insight into the Roman public's penchant for watching violence and death in the arena. At its core, the Roman Empire was a warring society. It was able to expand to cover much of Europe and northern Africa by fighting violently, conquering native groups, and enslaving people. One theory about why gladiator fights were so successful is that they helped prepare citizens for future bloody battles. In addition, most ancient civilizations had no concept of **human rights** and did not view slavery or the death of enslaved people or criminals as wrong.

Still, the public enjoyed watching the spectacles, although change was on the horizon thanks to a new religion, Christianity, which slowly but surely gained followers throughout the empire.

The founder of Christianity, Jesus Christ, lived in Galilee, a Roman province, and was crucified by Roman soldiers in 33 CE. Christianity presented a threat to Roman leaders because Christians proclaimed adherence to one God, not to many gods as the Romans did. Christians refused to worship the emperor and preached about love, understanding, compassion, and human rights—values sorely lacking at gladiator fights. Roman leaders did not appreciate criticism from Christians and often put them to death. In fact, Christians' deaths became part of gladiator fight pre-festivities, as emperors sometimes ordered Christians or people of other faiths thrown to wild animals in arenas in front of thousands of cheering spectators.

Despite the persecution, Christianity gained strength. Each time Christians were put to death in the arena, they won more converts, who realized that the actions they witnessed were at odds with what their new friends were preaching. In 312, the Roman emperor Constantine (c. 274–337) embraced Christianity and declared it the state religion. In 323, he banned gladiator combats and sentenced criminals and captives to hard labor instead. Constantine found it hard to enforce his own ban, however, as his desire to end gladiator fights was at odds with his desire to gain public favor. As a result, the fights continued. In 367, Emperor Valentinian I (321–375) declared that Christians would not be forced to enroll in gladiator training schools, and in

IN 312, THE ROMAN EMPEROR CONSTANTINE (C. 274–337) EMBRACED CHRISTIANITY AND DECLARED IT THE STATE RELIGION.

399, Emperor Honorius (384–423) closed all gladiator schools. But fights continued.

Legend has it that an unfortunate and dramatic event put an end to all gladiator games. During a contest in 404, a Christian monk named Telemachus (c. 300s–404) jumped down from the stands into the Colosseum, despite the sharp swords and heavy armor swinging in his way. He fought to separate the two contestants, and his actions threw the crowd into a fury. They rose from their seats and leaped down into the arena. The angry mob chased down

Telemachus and killed him. Honorius, who witnessed the ugly spectacle, declared an end to all gladiator contests.

This came at a time when Rome was on the descent. In 410, **barbarian** warriors sacked the city. Later, a powerful earthquake damaged the Colosseum. Just seven decades after Honorius's ban, the Roman Empire, corrupted by power and out of money, disintegrated. No one held the power to keep gladiators captive any longer. The era of the gladiator was over.

Yet, the gladiator's lifestyle lives on today in popular fiction and film. In his 2005 novel *Sand of the Arena,* James Duffy recreates the world of gladiators as a fighter named Taurus rises in the gladiator ranks and soon finds himself face-to-face with his nemesis in a Roman amphitheater. A similar novel, *Song of the Gladiator* by Paul Doherty, features a gladiator who becomes a pawn in a

Actor Russell Crowe, from the movie *Gladiator*

Water Battles

Occasionally, an especially ambitious emperor made plans for a great sea battle. This fight took place not in an actual sea, but in either an artificial lake or the amphitheater itself. Sometimes thousands of gladiators participated, and the event drew tens of thousands of spectators. The emperor might release sharks or other dangerous sea creatures to make the event more dramatic. The gladiators poised themselves on large wooden boats that were sleek and slim to more easily cut through the water. The boats maneuvered side-by-side, and gladiators used spears or bows and arrows to attack their opponents.

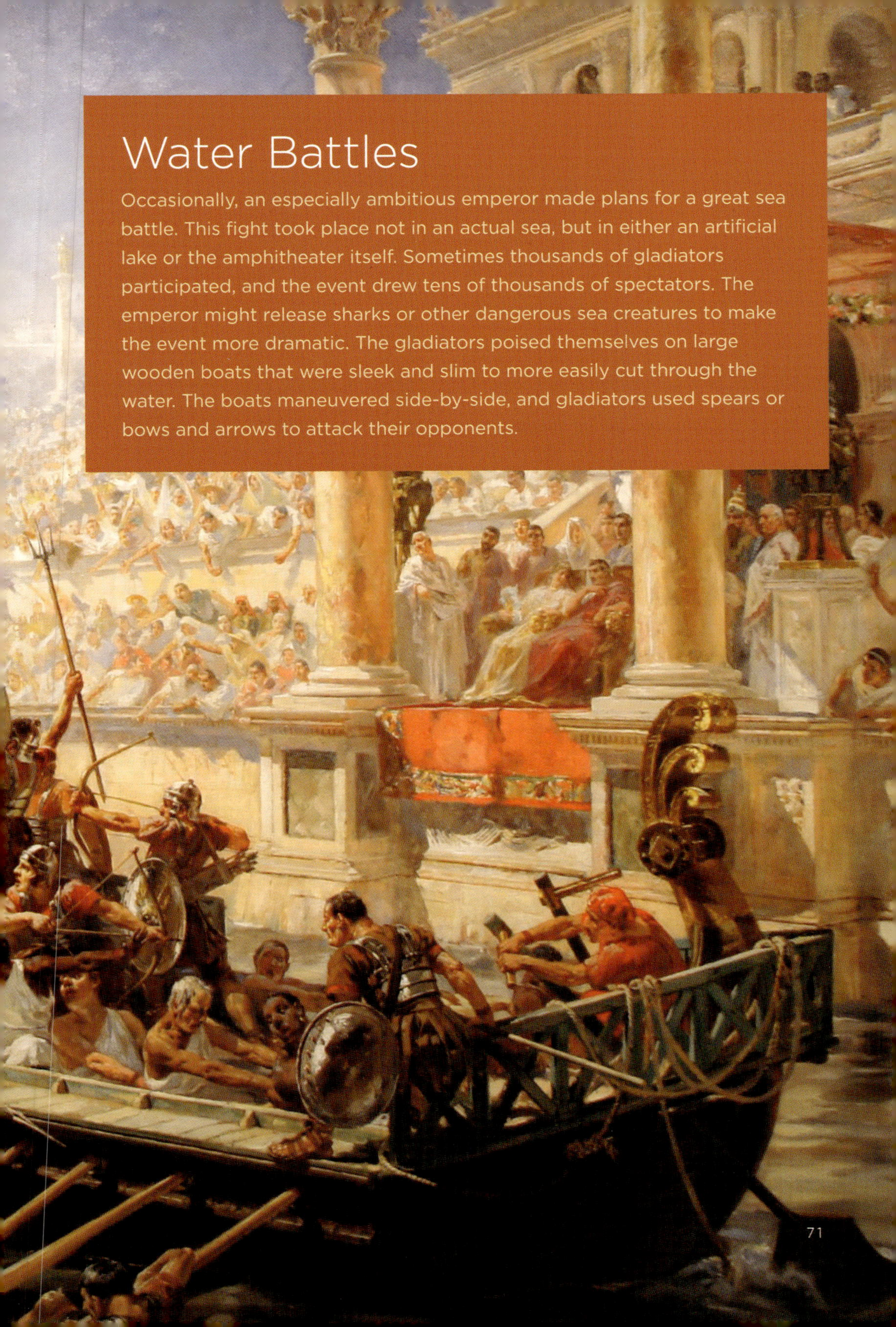

vast betting network. On television, the topic of gladiators enjoyed a resurgence in the 1990s with *American Gladiators*, a game show on which contestants were chosen to "battle" the show's stable of athletic "gladiators." Contestants and gladiators competed in a number of challenges that emphasized strength, speed, and agility.

Gladiators have also proved a popular subject on the silver screen. In 1960, director Stanley Kubrick brought the ancient story of the famous slave revolt of Spartacus to life. Starring some of the biggest actors in Hollywood at the time, *Spartacus* focuses not only on the brute strength of the gladiators but on the intellectual ideas behind their revolt. The movie is based on a novel of the same name. More recently, the era of gladiators came vividly to life on the movie screen in 2024's *Gladiator II*, a sequel to 2000's *Gladiator*, starring Russell Crowe. In both films, director

Ridley Scott presents a view of gladiatorial Rome never seen before, with intense sword fights and grisly battle scenes.

Many elements of gladiatorial life can be found in today's sports world. In hundreds of sports arenas, tough, strong athletes enter to the deafening cheers of their fans. Boxers perhaps most closely duplicate the hand-to-hand fighting of gladiators. Professional wrestlers, with their outrageous behavior and costumes, surely are modeled after similar crowd-pleasing gladiators of years past. Like winning gladiators, the best modern athletes are exalted.

Today, tough athletes not only fight as boxers and wrestlers, but in some places, they fight as gladiators, reenacting ancient gladiatorial battles without the blood and violence. A Jordanian company called RACE (Roman Army and Chariot Experience) has returned "gladiators" to the ancient arena in the city of Jerash, where audiences sit in the same seats as did ancient crowds. The rules are much the same, and the crowd gets to decide the fate of the fighters with a ceremonial thumbs-up or thumbs-down. In this era, though, even a gladiator who receives a thumbs-up gets to leave the arena alive.

Although such reenactments help to preserve the gladiator age, today bloody gladiator battles to the death have retreated into the dark recesses of history. No civilized society would dare let humans slay one another in an arena filled with thousands of cheering spectators. The gladiators of 2,000 years ago represent a time gone by, a time when poor and rich alike ventured out of their homes and drew together for public entertainment. Before professional sports, before movies, television, and music, there were gladiators.

Studying Bones

Scientists who discovered an ancient gladiator graveyard near Smyrna in Turkey stumbled upon clues pointing to the fighters' diet. By looking at the bones, scientists concluded that gladiators survived on a mostly vegetarian diet, consisting of large amounts of barley, **fennel**, and beans. Scientists also guessed that gladiators fought barefoot because their foot bones appeared enlarged. The bones also indicated that gladiators put on weight before combat and had a higher **bone density** than the average person. Although artwork generally shows physically bulky gladiators, this may have been more a reflection of their image than of their actual size.

Selected Bibliography

Beck, Melinda. "Did Women Fight as Gladiators in Ancient Rome?" History. April 12, 2024. https://www.history.com/news/women-gladiators-ancient-rome.

Futrell, Alison. *Blood in the Arena: The Spectacle of Roman Power.* Austin, Texas: University of Texas Press, 1997.

Harper, Kyle. *The Fate of Rome: Climate, Disease, and the End of an Empire.* Princeton, N.J.: Princeton University Press, 2017.

Larman, Alexander. "The Brutal History behind Gladiator 2's Flooded Colosseum Sea Battles." *The Telegraph.* July 10, 2024. https://www.telegraph.co.uk/films/0/gladiator-2-trailer-real-history-colosseum-sea-battles.

Newcomb, Tim. "Archaeologists Uncovered the Tomb of a Roman Gladiator—but the Gladiator Was Nowhere to Be Found." *Popular Mechanics.* October 14, 2024. https://www.popularmechanics.com/science/archaeology/a62569370/roman-gladiator-tomb-uncovered.

Nossov, Konstantin. *Gladiator: The Complete Guide to Ancient Rome's Bloody Fighters.* Guilford, Conn.: Lyons Press, 2009, 2011.

Glossary

acquit — to declare a person accused of a crime "not guilty"; an acquittal is usually granted by a jury or judge in a courtroom setting

agility — the ability to move with quickness and grace

barbarian — a member of a Germanic group that came down from the north to sack Rome in the fifth century CE

bone density — the weight of minerals in a bone; bone density determines how strong a bone is and how vulnerable it is to fractures; the higher the measurement, the stronger the bone

dehumanize — to deprive people of human qualities as a way to make them feel or seem less than human

democratic — related to a system of government that favors equality and decision-making by the people or by representatives elected by the people

dictator — a person given complete power and authority who often rules oppressively and does not take into account input from the people

fennel a type of herb that is part of the carrot family and possesses a strong odor and taste

forum a public square where some of the first gladiator fights took place; later replaced by amphitheaters

griffin a mythical animal with the head and wings of an eagle and the body, hind legs, and tail of a lion

harem a group of women who belong to and serve just one man; usually they live in a separate part of the man's large house or estate

human rights rights granted fundamentally to all humans, such as freedom from unfair imprisonment, torture, or death

nobleman an important man who ranked high within society; often noblemen were wealthy, well-respected, and came from a long line of nobility

noose a piece of rope with a loose knot that can be tightened when wrapped around an object; when looped around the neck, it can result in strangulation

opium a narcotic drug taken from the dried juice of poppy seeds; it has a brownish appearance, a bitter taste, and is addictive

reprieve the delay or cancellation of a punishment that's about to happen; usually granted by someone in power

senate the supreme council of the Roman Empire, where decisions were voted upon and passed by majority rule

stimulant a drug that temporarily increases a person's body activity or function; stimulants make users feel as if they are more awake

Websites

10 Things You May Not Know About Roman Gladiators

https://www.history.com/news/10-things-you-may-not-know-about-roman-gladiators

Discover cool facts about the famed fighters.

Ancient Roman Gladiators

https://www.thecolosseum.org/gladiators

Find out more about gladiator types, training, and fights.

The Roman Empire in the First Century

https://www.pbs.org/empires/romans/index.html

Explore what life was like in the early Roman Empire.

Index